Also by Natasha D. Frazier

Devotionals

The Life Your Spirit Craves

Not Without You

The Life Your Spirit Craves for Mommies

Not Without You Prayer Journal

Fiction

Love, Lies & Consequences

Through Thick & Thin: Love, Lies & Consequences Book 2

Shattered Vows: Love, Lies & Consequences Book 3

Kairos: The Perfect Time for Love

Out of the Shadows: Love, Lies & Consequences Book 4

Non-fiction

How Long Are You Going to Wait?

Copyright © 2020 by Natasha D. Frazier
Published by Encouraging Works
Printed by Lightning Source, Inc.

All rights reserved. No portion of this book may be used in any form without the written permission of the publisher.

Printed in the United States of America.

ISBN: 978-0-9994496-4-6

Scripture quotations marked NIV are taken from the *Holy Bible, New International Version*®. NIV®. Copyright © 1973, 1978, 1984, 2011 by International Bible Society. Used by permission of Zondervan Publishing House. All rights reserved.

Scripture quotations marked NKJV are taken from the *New King James Version*. Copyright © 1982, 1992 by Thomas Nelson, Inc. Used by permission. All rights reserved.

Scripture quotations marked NLT are taken from the *Holy Bible, New Living Translation,* copyright © 1996. Used by permission of Tyndale House Publishers, Inc., Wheaton Illinois 60189, U.S.A. All rights reserved.

Edited by Cheryl Molin

For autographed copies, please visit:
www.natashafrazier.com

Note from the Author

I don't think there has ever been a more perfect time for the release of this Bible study. Given all that's happening in our world now, it is important for God's children to understand that He still loves us and pursues our hearts, no matter the situation.

My prayer is that, by the end of this study, you'll see God at work in your life drawing you closer to Him even in the most unlikely situations.

The parables of the lost sheep, lost coin, and prodigal son are excellent examples of how God would have sent Jesus to die on the cross even if it were only you who needed salvation — that's how precious you are to Him!

Much love & many blessings,

Natasha

Dedicated to you

Acknowledgements

Honestly, I feel like a broken record when it comes to thanking those who have supported my work over the years. However, as repetitive as it may be, I must give thanks to my Father in Heaven who has given me the courage, ability, and ideas to write.

My husband, Eddie, who has supported my vision and passion for writing — thank you!

Mom, my biggest cheerleader, I've come this far because of your guidance, love, and support. Amber and Courtney, I love you both. To my Dad, Stepdad, and Aunt Rosie, thank you for all that you've contributed. Your love and sacrifice do not go unnoticed.

My soul sisters, Tiera, Toccara, and Shenitra, your friendship and encouragement is immeasurable.

The 5aithful, 5abulous, 5ive book club — you will always get a special shoutout from me because of your support. You ladies rock!

Readers, thank you for supporting my writing journey, whether it's reading, writing reviews, or telling others about my books, I appreciate you.

Cheryl, my dearest editor, without you, my work wouldn't shine as bright. Thank you!

Pursuit

Exploring God's endless quest for my heart

NATASHA D. FRAZIER

Pursuit

Moses

Read: Exodus 2 and 3

Meditational thought: What can I learn about God's pursuit of me through Moses' story?

Moses was set apart at birth. When Pharaoh put out an order to throw all the Israelite baby boys in the Nile River, Moses was saved by Pharaoh's daughter and his sister (Exodus 2:5). Years later, he fled to Midian after killing an Egyptian who was beating up an Israelite. While in Midian, he married Zipporah and started a family. Now here is Moses out living his life, tending his father-in-law's flock, when he has a God encounter: the burning bush (Exodus 3:2).

God appeared to Moses in the form of a bush that was engulfed in blazing fire, yet it wasn't burning up. Of course, Moses, like most of us would probably have been, was curious. He had to get closer to see what was happening. *Why isn't the bush burning?* When Moses walked closer to the bush, God began speaking to him, calling him by name.

Pursuit

One thing that amazes me is the confirmation that God knows each of us by name, just as He did Moses. He called Moses out to give him an assignment. In the midst of Moses living an ordinary life, forty years after he fled from Egypt, God pursued him (Acts 7:30). This lets us know that Moses, from birth, was set apart for God's purpose, as each of us is. We may not be called to lead a nation of people out of Egypt, but there are people within our sphere of influence who need to know God in a more intimate way.

Who in your life needs to know Christ?

_____
_____
_____
_____
_____

Moses was alone when he encountered the burning bush. So many of us are afraid to be alone, yet alone time with God is what we need for greater intimacy. Technology has become such a huge distraction: TVs, cellphones, computers, video games, etc. We become so immersed in those things that we don't leave room for time alone with God. By the time we're powering down the electronics, we're heading to bed.

I'm not sure Moses was alone so that he could experience God, but we need to take time to be alone. God pursued Moses in his solitude.

Pursuit

Solitude helps us to focus on God's voice so that we may hear Him clearly. Times are much different than they were back then, and life is not as simple, so we must be even more intentional about our time with God.

When God called to Moses, his response was, "Here I am." Then the Lord introduced Himself. For God to introduce Himself suggests that Moses didn't know who He was. When we encounter God's presence, we are introduced to His salvation, His goodness, His mercy, His sovereignty, His power at work in our lives, and more than anything, His love for us.

After God introduced Himself, He gave Moses an assignment. It isn't until we get into God's intimate presence and get to know who He is through Scripture that we can learn what He is asking of us. How else would we know He is leading us to do anything if we don't know Him or His voice? There is no way around it. Intimacy with God is a must.

→ Read Exodus 3:1–10

As a natural human response, Moses replies to God's assignment with his disqualifications. My friend, as with Moses, God knows you. After all, He is pursuing you and has been doing so your entire life. You are His child and He knows what you are capable of accomplishing. He knows what's inside of you, all of the talents and spiritual gifts, and even all the limitations, because He gave them to you for His purposes.

One thing I simply adore about God's call and pursuit of Moses is that God had a response to combat every reason that Moses thought he wasn't qualified to lead the children of Israel out of Egypt. When Moses asked God, "Who am I to appear before Pharaoh or to lead Your people out of Egypt," God said, "I will be with you." Let's think about this for a moment. God was asking him to appear before the highest official in Egypt to tell him to let God's people go. This could have gone badly for Moses because he could have been captured and made a slave or even put to death. Remember Pharaoh had the highest authority; he could have given the word to have Moses killed and that could have been the end of that story. Recall that Pharaoh previously wanted him dead for killing an Egyptian before he fled Egypt. God's response shifted the focus from Moses to Himself. This is something we should take note of, because without Him, we can do nothing (John 15:5). Sometimes we simply have to remove ourselves from the situation, as hard as that may seem.

Moses protested again. "Who should I say sent me?" Of course, God had an answer for this: I AM WHO I AM.

Moses protested yet again, asking what if they didn't believe that God sent him. This is a natural response. I'd probably be concerned as well. God is asking him to leave his comfort zone to go to a place where the people knew him and his sin to do something he has never done. However, God already had that part figured out as well.

When we think of things we learn about God in the Old Testament, we tend to separate them from the present, but the Bible tells us that God doesn't change. He is the same today as He was yesterday, last year, and back in the times of the Old Testament. These words are given to us so that we may have a greater understanding of who God is. In knowing this, if God had His plan for Moses figured out and the answer to all his questions and concerns, surely, He does for you and me as well.

Pursuit

Moses went to Pharaoh and delivered God's message and of course Pharaoh didn't listen. In fact, Moses received the opposite response from him. Pharaoh got upset and made life worse for the Israelites. Now everyone is upset with Moses, both Pharaoh and the Israelites. Moses gets discouraged like any of us would be when the plan doesn't work out as we perceived it would. "God, I listened to Your voice and followed through with Your plan, but this didn't turn out like I expected."

Can you recall a situation when this happened to you? What was your response? What encouraged you to keep going?

_____
_____
_____
_____
_____
_____
_____
_____
_____
_____
_____
_____

We know the story. God sent Moses back to Pharaoh multiple times, allowing the Egyptians to endure ten plagues, until Pharaoh finally decided to let God's people go.

Pursuit

This is a good illustration of God's pursuit of His people. He doesn't stop pursuing our hearts because things don't work out. He doesn't even stop pursuing us when we go our own way. Thinking back to the story of God bringing His chosen people out of Egypt, surely God is almighty and could have released His people sooner, yet He didn't. He used the plagues to demonstrate His power.

Has God allowed something to happen in your life to demonstrate His power while in pursuit of you? Explain.

_____
_____
_____
_____
_____
_____
_____
_____
_____
_____
_____
_____
_____
_____

Pursuit

What can we learn about God's pursuit of us through Moses' story?

_____
_____
_____
_____
_____
_____
_____
_____

Remember that God will use peculiar situations to get our attention. Things are not always as they seem. Have patience and trust in God's holy plan.

Pursuit

The midwives, however, _____ God and did not do what the king of Egypt had told them to do; they let the boys live. (Exodus 1:17 NIV)

Read Exodus 3:12, 14–22. What does God answer for every excuse we have?

Read Exodus 3:12. When I am afraid or uncertain, what does God remind me of His character?

Read Exodus 4:2. God has given us what we need. What encouragement does God give to Moses that will also help me?

Read Exodus 5:2. What does the Scripture teach about the correlation of obeying and following God?

Pursuit

He revealed his _____ to Moses and His deeds to the people of Israel. (Psalm 103:7 NLT)

David

Read: 1 Samuel 16

Meditational Thought: What can I learn about God's pursuit of me through David's story?

David is my favorite person to study from the Old Testament because his story is inspiring and akin to ours. It is evident that God pursued him. From what we learn about him in 1 Samuel 16, he wasn't out campaigning to be king; he was minding his business taking care of the sheep and goats. And yet, God sent Samuel to seek out one of Jesse's sons, David, to be the next king of Israel.

God literally pursues David to become the next king of Israel, sending Samuel on a journey to find David. At the time Samuel didn't know who he was looking for; he was simply listening to the voice of God and following His lead. God told him to go and he went, risking getting found out by Saul, who was the current king. What do you think Saul would have done had he known that Samuel was on his way to anoint the next king because God had rejected him?

Pursuit

In a remarkably familiar passage of Scripture, 1 Samuel 16:7, God instructs Samuel not to judge by outward appearance because God looks at the heart of man. That is the one I'd like to focus on here. When the Holy Spirit taps us on the shoulder, we often respond with hesitation, fear, or disbelief, because we don't see others or ourselves the way that God sees us. We're often focused on the things that we can see, but God can see the invisible, including the condition of our hearts. Because we can be so misguided in our thinking, we miss God's gentle nudging of our hearts.

Hesitation – "I'll do this Lord, but . . ." can lead to procrastination and never getting anything done at all.

Fear – "God, I can't do *that*. I don't have the time, resources, or background."

Disbelief sounds a lot like, "God didn't say that." I did not hear a small quiet voice speaking to me. God wouldn't ask that of me!

In spite of anything you or I can come up with, God still chooses us in spite of our hearts. He isn't looking at our stature, haircuts, houses, cars, shoes, outfits, makeup, or any other thing that describes or defines our outward appearance.

Who loves Me? Who desires to do My will? Who will listen to My voice? I believe those are the things God looks at when choosing us for assignments to draw people unto Him.

So the next time you question whether or not God has called you for a task because someone else "looks" as if they'd be a better fit than you, think again and remember 1 Samuel 16:7.

Pursuit

Can you recall God choosing you for a specific task? What was the task and how did you respond?

_____
_____
_____
_____
_____
_____
_____
_____
_____
_____

David is most known for two accounts from the Bible: killing the Philistine giant and his adultery with Bathsheba. When David told Saul not to worry about the Philistine because he will go fight him, Saul thought David was out of his mind. Saul judged David by his outward appearance. David was much smaller than the soldiers in Saul's army and especially the giant Philistine, plus David had no experience fighting in wars. The armor was too big for him and he wasn't planning to use a sword or spear. Surely it seemed he was on his way to death; however, Saul agreed to let him fight the giant Philistine.

While Saul was concerned for David's safety, David most certainly was not. He had fought animals in his capacity as a shepherd and he believed the *same* God who gave him victory in the past would also give him victory over the Philistines.

David believed something that we all should have buried in our hearts and minds: if God did it once, He has the power to do it again. He is the same God today as He was yesterday, as He'll be tomorrow (Hebrews 13:8). We must learn and rest in that truth because that is key in understanding how God pursues us. He wants us to trust that if He has moved in our lives before, He will do it again.

When you consider Hebrews 13:8, is there something in your life right now that you need to confess this truth over? In what situation do you need to be reminded that God has not changed? Write a prayer here confessing this truth.

_____
_____
_____
_____
_____
_____
_____
_____
_____
_____
_____
_____

Before David made a move on Goliath, he said something particularly important. First Samuel 17:47b NKJV says, "For the battle is the Lord's." David believed and trusted that God would give him victory for such a great task. We must also remember that the battle we fight is spiritual and belongs to the Lord. It's not against flesh and blood . . . and He has given us what we need to fight (the Word).

What battle are you attempting to fight with the wrong weapon?

_____
_____
_____
_____

Search the Scriptures. What do the Scriptures say about that situation?

_____
_____
_____
_____
_____
_____
_____

Pursuit

After David defeated the Philistines, he continued to win battles for King Saul. See, Saul became jealous and continued to send David to war because he wanted him killed, but Saul didn't know or understand that by doing that he was assisting David in becoming well known and preparing him to be the next king—quite the opposite of what he wanted to do. Saul knew that God was with David but that didn't stop him from trying to destroy David. You and I aren't much different. The enemy knows that God is with us and there isn't anything he can do to separate us from the love of God (Romans 8:31–39), but that won't stop him from trying to get in our head. He knows God is in love with us and pursuing us for His purpose. It's time we know it too!

Satan knows that God has a purpose for you, but that won't stop him from trying to destroy you. How has the enemy been getting in your head lately? Search the Scripture and write down what God's Word says about it.

_____
_____
_____
_____
_____
_____

There are consequences for our sin, but as we learned from David's adultery with Bathsheba, God forgives and cleanses us of our sins, and He can/will still use us for His divine purpose. As a result of

David sleeping with Bathsheba, she became pregnant, but as a consequence for David's sin, the child died. Now if you're unfamiliar with this story, David also tried to cover up his sin by attempting to trick her husband into sleeping with her so that it would seem as if he was the father of the child, and not David. When that didn't work, he arranged to have him killed (2 Samuel 11). Insane! God remained with David, gave him victory in countless battles, blessed him with more children (including King Solomon), and inspired David to write most of the book of Psalms, which still inspires us today.

Are you allowing your shame from sin to hinder your relationship with God? If so, why? Study Romans 8. What do you learn from this chapter?

___
___
___
___
___
___
___
___
___
___

Pursuit

Does God's pursuit of David remind you of His pursuit of you? How?

_____
_____
_____
_____
_____
_____
_____
_____
_____
_____

Pursuit

Read 1 Samuel 16:2-3. What can you learn about trusting God?

But the Lord said to Samuel, "Do not consider his appearance or his height, for I have rejected him. The Lord does not look at the things people look at. People look at the_____, but the Lord looks at the _____." (1 Samuel 16:7 NIV)

Read 1 Samuel 16:10-13. What does the Bible teach about who God chooses?

In everything he did he had great _____, because the Lord was with him. . (1 Samuel 18:14 NIV)

I will _____ you and _____ you in the way you should go;
I will _____ you with my loving eye on you. (Psalm 32:8 NIV)

18

Pursuit

Jesus Christ is the _____ yesterday and today and forever. (Hebrews 13:8 NIV)

Gideon

Read: Judges 6 -7

Meditational Thought: Even when I am afraid, God still pursues me.

Gideon was threshing wheat at the bottom of a winepress when the Lord pursued him. Threshing normally took place out in the open with grain particles flying everywhere, but Gideon was essentially working in the bottom of a pit, in isolation and hiding, which had to be uncomfortable. He was hiding because the Midianites had been taking food from the Israelites and leaving them to starve. Gideon figured if he could do his work in the bottom of the winepress, he could preserve food and no one would see him. I imagine no one saw him, and he was able to stay out of sight of everyone but the Most High God. See Judges 6:1–6.

Gideon threshing wheat in a winepress is a great example of the fact that it doesn't matter where you are, God can reach you. When God is in pursuit of you, nothing can get in the Almighty's way, not even you in a self-dug pit.

Have you rejected the thought of God speaking to you because of where you are in life? Why?

_____
_____
_____
_____
_____
_____

When the angel of the Lord told Gideon that God was with him, he questioned the angel because of his people's present circumstances. If God is with us, why has all of this happened to us? (Judges 6:13).

When things aren't working in your favor, do you doubt God leading you? Doubt He's speaking to you? Can you recall a specific situation when things weren't working well, and you later realized that God was speaking to you through that situation?

_____
_____
_____
_____
_____
_____

Pursuit

_____
_____
_____
_____
_____
_____

Do you *hide* from God? Do you avoid God's voice speaking to you? What is the result of that? Have you found that it's futile?

_____
_____
_____
_____
_____
_____
_____
_____
_____

When God pursued Gideon, He gave him a command to go with the strength he had because God was sending him. This can be scary, especially when you feel like you aren't qualified. Besides, in today's times angels aren't sitting down with us or appearing to us face-to-face, so we question if we really heard God, are qualified, or have the strength to carry out whatever the Holy Spirit is leading us to do. When we spend time with God, we learn His voice and we must trust that He has given us the mental and spiritual strength and lined up provision to carry out His plans.

"But Lord," Gideon replied, "how can I rescue Israel? My clan is the weakest in the whole tribe of Manasseh, and I am the least in my entire family!" (Judges 6:15 NLT)

What was your response the last time the Holy Spirit nudged you about completing a specific task? Did you try to talk yourself or even God out of it, like Gideon?

_____
_____
_____
_____
_____
_____
_____
_____
_____
_____

Pursuit

Do you think Gideon's concerns were valid?

_____
_____
_____
_____

Negative self-talk and doubt will destroy our faith and have us forgetting the power of God. When God told Gideon to go, he basically said to God that he was at the bottom of the totem pole. How could he be the one to rescue Israel when he was so unimportant? I guarantee that you are much harder on yourself than God is, which is why He pursues you to show you that He loves you, you matter, and that you're valuable to Him. He doesn't care about the title you have in your church or at your job, He wants you. No matter how little you may see in yourself, God sees you as His masterpiece whom He designed who fits perfectly into His master plan to win the hearts of those under your influence.

What have you talked yourself out of because you feel you aren't good enough? Or you don't have the right specific title or the right influence?

_____
_____
_____
_____

Pursuit

Do you recognize a pattern of negative self-talk in your life? If so, what are they?

_____
_____
_____
_____
_____
_____

Remember that negative self-talk is from the enemy because he doesn't want you to do God's will. If Satan can kill your confidence, steal your dreams, and destroy your faith, he has accomplished his purpose in your life.

Despite what the enemy tries to do, remember that God is much bigger and His thoughts and ways much higher than ours. (See Isaiah 55.) For every "but" and excuse that you or I can come up with, God has an answer. He is with us. God's response to Gideon's doubt was a reminder that He was with him and that everything would be fine. In fact, God told him that it would be like Gideon was fighting against one man when he went up against the Midianite army (Judges 6:16).

Can you recall a time when you stepped out on faith to do a specific task, one that you thought was much too hard for you to accomplish on your own? What reminders did God show you along the way to prove that He was with you?

Pursuit

_____
_____
_____
_____
_____
_____
_____
_____
_____
_____

"Show me a sign." Gideon was convinced that God had the wrong person because he was least in his family, so he needed proof that God was really talking to him.

How many times have you asked God to show you a sign? When He showed you a sign, what did you do? How did you respond?

_____
_____
_____
_____
_____

Pursuit

Do you think Gideon had the right idea in asking God for a sign?

_____
_____
_____
_____
_____

I believe Gideon's question was valid. After all, he was being tasked with a huge assignment. Whenever we believe we're being led to do a task, we want to be sure that it's God and that He's going to be with us, leading us along the way, so we should start with a prayer to confirm the direction God would have us go. If you're unsure of God's voice, know that anything of God will not contradict God's Word (test the spirit by the Spirit, 1 John 4:1). Ask yourself if it glorifies the kingdom of God. Do you have any selfish motives?

Just as God proved to Gideon that He was in pursuit of him in Judges 6:20–21, God always confirms whatever He says. As God pursues us, He gives us "signs" even when we don't ask for them—He's awesome like that!

Even though God's pursuit of us can sometimes lead us into doing something outside of our comfort zone, we can trust that He knows our abilities, He knows the future, and we can trust His plan. We must, however, make ourselves available for the task(s).

Pursuit

Do it afraid. After God proved to Gideon that He would be with him, He gave Gideon a specific set of instructions in Judges 6:25–27. Gideon was afraid of the town and what his family would think, so he did what God asked him to do, but in secret, at night. Sometimes we have to do it afraid. I'm not sure what doing it afraid will look like for you, but I do know that you must move, take action, and answer God's voice that's calling out to you to do a specific thing.

What is it that God has been asking of you that has you afraid? Will you commit to doing it afraid as we learn from Gideon?

_____
_____
_____
_____
_____
_____
_____
_____
_____

What does "doing it afraid" look like for you?

_____
_____
_____
_____

Pursuit

Gideon got in the groove of walking with God more closely, but he still needed assurance. He asked God for two specific signs and God performed them exactly as Gideon asked to show that He was with Gideon. I believe God wants us to walk close enough with Him that we'll trust His Word.

Like Gideon, do you struggle with your faith and often ask God for signs? Why or why not?

Have you ever asked for a sign and God didn't give it? When you consider it now, did He give a sign and you missed it?

Pursuit

_____
_____
_____
_____
_____
_____
_____

    God doesn't hold our fear against us. Oftentimes He will show us that we have no reason to be afraid. God speaks in many ways (prayers, dreams, visions, sermons, His Word) and sometimes He will allow you a glimpse of the victory. You'll trust and do the work of God's kingdom in confidence. For Gideon, in Judges 7:1–13, God allowed him to hear the interpretation of someone else's dream (the enemy in this case). As a reminder to you, the enemy knows the battle has been won, but that won't stop him from planting fear in your heart and mind. Stand strong on the fact that God pursued you is going before you in whatever He is leading you to do.

Pursuit

Read Judges 6:11-16. What does the Bible teach me about God's strength?

Jehovah-Shalom means the Lord is _____. (Judges 6:24)

"For my _____ are not your thoughts, neither are your ways my ways," declares the Lord. "As the heavens are higher than the earth, so are my ways _____ than your ways and my thoughts than your thoughts. (Isaiah 55:8-9 NIV)

So shall My Word be that goes forth from My mouth; It shall not return to Me _____, But it shall accomplish what I please, and it shall _____ in the thing for which I sent it. (Isaiah 55:11 NKJV)

Read Ephesians 1:4. What does the Bible teach me about God choosing me?

Pursuit

After studying Gideon's encounters with God, are there situations where I can clearly see God's pursuit of me?

Saul/Paul

Read Acts 7:54–8:3, Acts 9:1–31

Meditational Thought: Am I too messed up for God to pursue me?

Saul (who later became known as Paul) was one of the biggest persecutors of the church and Christians, yet God still pursued him. If anything seems like a reason for God to throw someone away, I'd think that would be it, but God's thoughts aren't like ours and Saul's story proves that God can transform and use anyone. If you think you're too messed up for God to even be remotely interested in pursuing you, think again!

We first hear of Saul in Acts 7:58 when the Jewish leaders stoned Stephen, a man who was described as being full of God's grace and power, performing miracles. Saul witnessed his death. In fact, we learn that Saul was going everywhere to destroy the church. He went from house to house, dragging out both men and women to throw them into prison (Acts 8:3). Their only crime was believing in Jesus Christ as the Messiah.

Do you believe that there's something you've done that makes you unlovable by God? What is it? Why do you believe this act makes you unlovable?

_____
_____
_____
_____
_____
_____
_____
_____

God loves you in spite of your sins. (See John 3:16.) God knew our sin before Jesus died on the cross. Because of Jesus' blameless life and obedience up to and after the cross, God pursues us because He sees believers through the blood of Jesus.

In the midst of Saul carrying on His crusade against Christians, Jesus' pursuit of Saul was manifested by Jesus calling out to him from heaven. The Bible tells us that a light shone down and caused Saul to fall to the ground. When Jesus called out to him, Saul responded by calling Him Lord. Saul knew who was calling out to Him. I don't think he was utterly confused when He heard Jesus' voice. I think that he lacked intimacy and wanted clarity. Many times, I believe we know when God is speaking to us, but if God's voice is leading us to do something for the kingdom that makes us uncomfortable, we respond in a similar manner as Saul, "Who are you? You can't be talking to me. You've got the wrong person. Surely that wasn't God speaking to me." God can give a thousand confirmations and we will continue to ask if He's talking to us or get stuck trying to discern His voice.

What is God's voice leading you to do today? Be specific.

_____
_____
_____
_____
_____
_____
_____

It is easier to discern God's voice when we know Him and have intimacy with Him. The more we spend time with Him, the greater intimacy we'll have, so when God speaks, we'll know and trust that it is His voice.

In Acts 9:5 (KJV), Jesus tells Saul that it is hard for him to kick against the pricks. God was telling Saul here that continuing to rebel against Him was not going to go well for him. Saul couldn't continue along the path of persecuting Christ followers and opposing ministers of the Gospel.

Pursuit

We may not go about it the way that Saul did when he persecuted the church, but to rebel against God's truths and laws or to get upset with a preacher or teacher of the Gospel because of rebuke is also kicking against the pricks. It's going against God's Word and truth when we know we're wrong. And yet, God will continue to pursue us so that we'll see the error of our ways and turn back to Him.

In what area of your life have you been intentionally disobeying God's Word?

_____
_____
_____
_____

In Acts 9:4, Jesus asked Saul why he was persecuting Him. That leads us to a question of conscience and to think about the root of the issue. Why am I doing this—and is it worth it to the detriment of peace with God?

Is your sin worth your peace with your Heavenly Father?

_____
_____
_____
_____
_____

Pursuit

This encounter that Saul had with Jesus changed his entire direction. He went from wanting to tear down anything that had to do with Jesus to recognizing his sin, being shaken and astonished, and asking Jesus "what would You have me do?" A mighty humbling self-less question. He went from serving others (priests and himself) to wanting to serve Jesus.

Write a prayer and ask Jesus, "What would you have me do?"

_____
_____
_____
_____
_____
_____
_____
_____
_____

The Lord didn't immediately tell Saul exactly what He wanted him to do for the kingdom; instead He instructed Saul to get up and go into the city and then he'd find out what he must do. When he stood up, he was blind. The men who were with him were speechless, as I think we all would have been in that situation. Let's think for a second about how Saul's encounter with God had an effect on them. In Acts 9:7, the Bible says they heard the voice but didn't see anyone.

Pursuit

When you encounter Jesus, how are those around you impacted?

_____
_____
_____
_____
_____
_____
_____
_____

Saul's reputation preceded him. The believers knew that he was on his way to bind them in chains and take them back to the chief priests, so they were afraid of him, including Ananias. Yet God used Ananias, a disciple in Damascus, to find Saul, lay hands on him to restore his sight, and allow Saul to be filled with the Holy Spirit. The Bible tells us that he was baptized. What a transformation! He did not stop there. He began preaching and teaching the Word of God! Wow!

What has your transformation through Christ Jesus led you to do?

_____
_____
_____
_____

Pursuit

Saul, also referred to as Paul after he began his missionary journey, traveled to preach and teach the Gospel of Jesus Christ and even wrote many of the books in the New Testament. You and I aren't writing books of the Bible, but we can make an impact on the kingdom of God. Saul/Paul is proof that an encounter with Jesus can change us for the betterment of God's eternal kingdom in spite of our past. In fact, Paul uses his past as a testimony to prove that if God can change him, God can change us too.

What is your testimony? Do you share it with others?

Pursuit

If God pursued Saul even in the midst of him persecuting Jesus Christ, how much more will He pursue you? God loves you beyond measure. See John 3:16.

Pursuit

Read Romans 8:35-39. What can separate me from God's love?

_____ never fails. (1 Corinthians 13:8 NIV)

And may you have the power to understand, as all God's people should, how wide, how long, how high, and how _____his love is. (Ephesians 3:18 NLT)

May you experience the _____, though it is too great to understand fully. Then you will be made complete with all the fullness of life and power that comes from God. (Ephesians 3:19 NLT)

And we have known and believed the _____ that God has for us. God is _____, and he who abides in _____ abides in _____, and God in him. (1 John 4:16 NKJV)

See what great _____ the Father has lavished on us, that we should be called children of God! And that is what we are! The reason the world does not know us is that it did not know him. (1 John 3:1 NIV)

Joseph, son of Jacob

Read: Genesis 37

Meditational thought: Can God pursue me through dreams?

In Genesis chapter 37, we are introduced to Jacob's favorite son, Joseph. Jacob, later called Israel, was father to twelve sons who became the tribes of Israel that we read about throughout the Old Testament. The Bible tells us in verse 9 that Joseph was Jacob's favorite son because he was born in Jacob's old age.

We first begin to see God's pursuit of Joseph through his dreams. God often spoke to Joseph through his dreams by showing him the future. Two specific dreams that Joseph had were that his brothers' bundles of grain would bow low before his bundle and that the sun, moon, and eleven stars bowed before him.

Pursuit

Has God spoken to you through dreams? What vision did He give you? What was your response?

_____
_____
_____
_____
_____
_____
_____

The Bible says that Joseph's brothers hated him because of how he talked about his dreams. This suggests that he could have been bragging a bit, especially given the fact that they didn't treat him well. This was his opportunity to boast, so he was likely adding fuel to the fire.

Although God showed Joseph his future through those dreams, it took many years before they materialized. Joseph wasn't ready and God already had a plan in place for how these things would happen. In Genesis 15:13, God told Abraham that He would bring His people to the Promised Land but that they would be in bondage for four hundred years before that. Joseph's story is intricate in facilitating God's plan. Joseph wasn't privy to God's complete thoughts; he only knew that the roles were going to shift, and his brothers were going to show him the respect he thought he deserved one day. Though we may know what God will do in our lives, He won't allow it to happen if we're not mature enough to handle it.

Is there something in your life that you're waiting for God to do? What is it? Could it be that God is waiting for you because you're not spiritually prepared? Would your focus shift away from Him if He answered this desire?

_____
_____
_____
_____
_____
_____
_____
_____
_____
_____
_____
_____

Joseph encountered pit stops even though he knew God had a greater plan for his life. Initially his brothers plotted to kill him but changed their minds and sold him into slavery. The Bible doesn't mention his faith, but being sold into slavery is a great time to wonder what was to become of his dreams.

Pursuit

When you encounter setbacks, how do you respond? Do you doubt God's pursuit of you when things don't work out the way you thought they would?

_____
_____
_____
_____
_____
_____
_____
_____
_____
_____

God can and will show you favor wherever you are. When Joseph was taken to Egypt, he was sold to Potiphar, an Egyptian officer who was captain of Pharaoh's guard. In Genesis 39:1, we learn that even though Joseph had to serve Potiphar, God was still with him. Though it was a terrible circumstance to have been sold into slavery, God showed Joseph favor where he was by giving him success even in that. This proves to us that no matter how bad our situation may seem, God can use it. He may show us favor as Joseph had, giving us peace, and even making us successful. One thing I believe is key is that we remain faithful to Him and continue to serve Him no matter what our situation looks like. Surely it can always be worse.

Pursuit

Genesis 39:6b–9 shows us that Potiphar's wife wanted to sleep with Joseph, but he chose to honor God. He said, "How could I do such a wicked thing? It will be a sin against God." High five Joseph! He kept God first in the midst of the temptation. However, Potiphar's wife lied by telling her husband that Joseph tried to rape her, so he was thrown in prison. He was punished for making the right choice.

Can you recall a situation you've had (or may still be in) that was not ideal, but God showed you favor anyway? Write it here.

_____
_____
_____
_____
_____
_____
_____
_____
_____
_____

How did that situation strengthen your relationship with God?

_____
_____
_____
_____

Pursuit

How can you recognize God at work in your life?

Write about a situation when you were punished for doing the right thing, making a choice that would honor God. Or perhaps you had a chance to make a good choice but you made an easy one instead. What was the end result? If given the opportunity, would you make the same choice today?

Pursuit

_____
_____
_____
_____
_____
_____
_____
_____
_____
_____

Even while Joseph was in prison, God remained faithful and showed Joseph favor. Not only was he serving time in prison, but he was serving time for a crime he did not commit. The Bible doesn't say how Joseph felt, but I'm sure we could imagine what it is like to suffer consequences for something we didn't do, or we've experienced something similar. In the midst of that, Joseph became the prison warden's favorite and was put in charge over the other prisoners and everything else that happened in the prison because of God's favor. No matter our circumstances, whether we be in a physical or mental prison, we can trust that God is there. And even in what seems like the worst of circumstances, God can help us through them. The unbearable becomes bearable. God had a plan for Joseph and this situation would not hinder it.

Pursuit

What is your prison and how is God at work within it?

_____
_____
_____
_____
_____
_____
_____

Joseph's gift was interpreting dreams. While in prison, he used his gift when two of Pharaoh's officials were thrown in prison and he was given watch over them. Do not allow your circumstances to dim the light of your gift. Wherever you are, use it, walk in it. If your gift is to sing, sing even in the worst of situations. If you have the gift of exhortation, lift up others in spite of what you're going through. Whatever your gift, use it to God's glory in spite of what's happening around you or to you. In fact, using your gift will shift your focus from your problems to God, which is enough to help change your mindset.

Both of Pharaoh's officials had dreams that required interpretation and Joseph understood and explained the dreams correctly. Joseph asked them to remember him when they were back in Pharaoh's service, and tell Pharaoh about him so that he would get out of prison, but they forgot about Joseph.

What is your spiritual gift? Do you exalt God even in the messiest of circumstances? If not, how does Joseph's story encourage you to do so?

_____
_____
_____
_____
_____
_____
_____
_____
_____
_____

→ Read Genesis 41

It took two years for Pharaoh's cup bearer to remember Joseph. Then he remembered Joseph's gift—interpreting dreams. Don't be discouraged if it seems like it's taking a long time for God to act on your behalf. Trust His plan. Pharaoh began to have dreams that bothered him, so he called for an interpreter and that's when the cupbearer remembered Joseph.

Pharaoh sent for Joseph and spoke about his dreams to him. Joseph interpreted them and gave a solution. As a result, here is what Genesis 41:37–44 NLT says,

Pursuit

Joseph's suggestions were well received by Pharaoh and his officials. So Pharaoh asked his officials, "Can we find anyone else like this man so obviously filled with the spirit of God?" Then Pharaoh said to Joseph, "Since God has revealed the meaning of the dreams to you, clearly no one else is as intelligent or wise as you are. You will be in charge of my court, and all my people will take orders from you. Only I, sitting on my throne, will have a rank higher than yours."

Pharaoh said to Joseph, "I hereby put you in charge of the entire land of Egypt." Then Pharaoh removed his signet ring from his hand and placed it on Joseph's finger. He dressed him in fine linen clothing and hung a gold chain around his neck. Then he had Joseph ride in the chariot reserved for his second-in-command. And wherever Joseph went, the command was shouted, "Kneel down!" So Pharaoh put Joseph in charge of all Egypt. And Pharaoh said to him, "I am Pharaoh, but no one will lift a hand or foot in the entire land of Egypt without your approval."

Wow! Look at how quickly Joseph's life turned around. At some point within those two years, I'm sure he felt forgotten and probably discouraged a time or two, but God continued to show Himself faithful.

Proverbs 18:16 (NKJV) says, "A man's gift makes room for him, and brings him before great men." How has your gift made room for you?

_____

_____

Pursuit

_____
_____
_____
_____
_____
_____
_____

Don't be discouraged by the length of time you've been waiting for God to act. How can God's faithfulness to Joseph encourage you in your wait?

_____
_____
_____
_____
_____
_____
_____
_____
_____

Joseph's story doesn't end there. Though Joseph was no longer a slave to Potiphar or a prisoner, God still hadn't allowed Joseph's dream (see Genesis 37) to come to pass. Joseph could've gotten comfortable with his position. I mean, he pretty much had everything: wealth, wife, prestige, but he didn't have his family. All of those things are good, but the most important thing is that God was with him and was far from done with the work He would do in and through Joseph's life.

Don't get too comfortable. Whether your current situation is good or bad, know that God is still at work in your life, helping you work out your salvation in Him (Philippians 2:12).

Have you become comfortable in your work, life, ministry, etc.? Are things going well but you're still waiting for God to answer a specific prayer? Write your prayer here. (Don't lose hope.)

_____
_____
_____
_____
_____
_____
_____

The famine happened just as God had revealed to Pharaoh through his dreams. Not only was there a famine in Egypt, but also in Canaan where Joseph's family lived. When Jacob heard that there was food in Egypt, he sent ten of his sons to buy grain. When they arrived, Joseph recognized them, but the Bible says they didn't know who he was.

Pursuit

Because of how they had treated Joseph years ago, he could have chosen to repay them by treating them badly, enslaving them, an eye for an eye or tooth for a tooth sort of thing, but he didn't harm them when it was in his power to do so. Instead he gave them free food by secretly returning their payment to them. In chapter 44, during the brothers' second trip to Egypt in which all eleven of Joseph's brothers traveled, we learn of Joseph planting his silver cup in Benjamin's (his younger brother) bag and demanding that he be left behind as a slave. Eventually Joseph revealed himself to his brothers and his response to their concern for what they did to him is powerful. Genesis 45:5–8 NLT says,

"But don't be upset, and don't be angry with yourselves for selling me to this place. It was God who sent me here ahead of you to preserve your lives. This famine that has ravaged the land for two years will last five more years, and there will be neither plowing nor harvesting. God has sent me ahead of you to keep you and your families alive and to preserve many survivors. So it was God who sent me here, not you! And he is the one who made me an adviser to Pharaoh—the manager of his entire palace and the governor of all Egypt.

This Scripture reminds us that God is in control even when it may not seem that way, but this is a fact that we must internalize and confess over our lives.

Unfortunately, Joseph had to endure an unpleasant journey before he was put in a position to save his entire family. When we're going through difficult times, the truth is that we don't know what the end will be or for what purpose we must endure certain things. However, we can

Pursuit

find hope in the fact that God loves us and chose us for it. He knows us and how we will respond, grow in relationship with Him, and lead others to Him. We may never discover the purpose we had to go through something or know whose life was changed by it in addition to ours. But we must trust God's knowledge, plan, and pursuit of us.

How does the story of Joseph's life encourage you?

_____
_____
_____
_____
_____
_____
_____
_____

Write about a time you were mistreated, and the situation later turned out in your favor. If it doesn't seem like it was in your favor, does Joseph's story help you to view it differently?

_____
_____
_____
_____
_____

Pursuit

Pursuit

The warden paid no attention to anything under Joseph's care, because the Lord was _____ Joseph and gave him _____ in whatever he did. (Genesis 39:23 NIV)

But those who hope in the Lord will _____ their strength. They will soar on wings like eagles; they will run and _____ grow weary, they will walk and not be _____. (Isaiah 40:31 NIV)

I can never escape from your _____. I can never get away from your _____. (Psalm 139:7 NLT)

You saw me before I was born. Every day of my life was _____ in your book. Every _____ was laid out before a single day had passed. (Psalm 139:16 NLT)

Until the time came to _____ the Lord tested Joseph's character. (Psalm 105:19 NLT)

Esther

Read: Esther 1 and 2

Meditational thought: God has positioned me for a special purpose.

Esther became queen after King Xerxes banished Queen Vashti for disrespecting him. He was hosting a huge banquet for the men in his kingdom for seven days, while Queen Vashti was hosting a banquet for the women in the royal palace. The Bible tells us that the king was high in spirits from wine and called for the queen so that everyone could gaze upon her beauty. Queen Vashti was not having it, so she refused to go to the king at his request. As a result, she lost her title and the king began his search for a new queen, a young virgin.

At the time of the king's decree to bring beautiful young virgins to the royal harem, Esther was living with her uncle, who adopted her as his daughter after her parents died. Whether Esther wanted to be included in this roundup or not, she didn't have much of a choice. Essentially she was snatched up from her normal everyday life to serve the king's needs.

Pursuit

Once she was brought to the royal harem, neither she nor any other young woman could see the king for an entire year. They had to be given a full year of beauty treatments, and then they were allowed to choose their clothes and jewelry before seeing the king. After spending the night with him, each woman would be moved to a second harem where his other concubines lived and couldn't go back to the king again unless he requested her by name. I don't know about you, but none of that appeals to me. However, the young women didn't have a choice so it doesn't matter if they liked the idea or not. Yet even in the midst of that, God was pursuing Esther. He had big plans for her to be used as a vessel to save her people.

A few key points here: 1. Esther was chosen as queen. This is important because she was a Jew and hid this fact because Jews were a despised group of people at this time. 2. Esther had to prepare a year to see the king. 3. Esther had favor. She was shown favor before she met the king and after she became queen (Esther 2:9).

In spite of your background, God can and will still choose you. What may seem as a hindrance to man can be a tool by God. Things are much different in God's hands.

Do you view your background as something that stands in the way of God using you? If so, why?

_____
_____
_____
_____

Pursuit

_____
_____
_____
_____

How do the passages in chapter 2 inspire you to know that God can use your background for His glory and to draw others closer to Him?

_____
_____
_____
_____
_____
_____
_____
_____

Esther had to prepare an entire year before she could see the king. That's three hundred and sixty-five whole days after she was chosen to go to the harem. Esther's wait was long, and sometimes our wait to get to where God is leading us can be long as well. However, during her wait, she wasn't idle; she spent that time preparing to see the king. There were specific things she had to do: six months of myrrh and oil treatments and another six months of fragrance treatments.

Pursuit

After her time of preparation, Esther was taken to King Xerxes. The Bible tells us that the king loved Esther more than any of the other women and declared her Queen.

While you wait for whatever you have been praying for or where God is leading you, what will you do to prepare? What are you preparing for?

_____
_____
_____
_____
_____
_____
_____
_____

Though your circumstances may not be ideal, look for God and His favor in the thick of it. How has God shown you favor where you are?

_____
_____
_____
_____
_____
_____

Pursuit

_____
_____
_____
_____

→Read Esther 3 and 4

Now the king wouldn't have anyone disrespecting him or his authority (recall what happened to Queen Vashti), so when Haman approached him about a certain group of people who refused to obey the king's laws, he agreed that they should die. It wasn't actually a group of people though, but only one person, Mordecai, a Jew, who wouldn't bow to Haman. As a result, Haman's ego was bruised and he sought revenge on every Jew, not just Mordecai. The king never asked who this group of people was. Perhaps he knew already. But he didn't know that Esther, the one he favored, was part of this group of people.

When Mordecai learned of the plan to execute the Jews, he went into mourning. Then Mordecai sent a message to Esther about the plan to destroy the Jews, and he asked her to go to the king and beg for mercy. The only problem with his plan is that Esther could be killed for entering the king's inner court uninvited. However, it seemed as if she was the Jews' only hope. In Esther 4:13–17 (NLT), the Bible says,

Mordecai sent this reply to Esther: "Don't think for a moment that because you're in the palace you will escape when all other Jews are killed. If you keep quiet at a time like this, deliverance and relief for the

Pursuit

Jews will arise from some other place, but you and your relatives will die. Who knows if perhaps you were made queen for just such a time as this?"

Then Esther sent this reply to Mordecai: "Go and gather together all the Jews of Susa and fast for me. Do not eat or drink for three days, night or day. My maids and I will do the same. And then, though it is against the law, I will go in to see the king. If I must die, I must die." So Mordecai went away and did everything as Esther had ordered him.

There's a lot going on here. Esther could potentially lose her life trying to save the lives of many others. She had been put in a difficult position, but she had to start somewhere: fasting and praying.

Do you fast and pray when you have to make difficult decisions? How do prayer and fasting affect your decision making? Do you enlist others to fast and pray with you?

_____
_____
_____
_____
_____
_____
_____
_____
_____
_____
_____

Can you identify a difficult situation when you felt like there was no way out? What did you do? What was the end result? How did your faith play a role in your decision-making? How does Esther's story inspire you to respond differently next time?

→Read Esther 5 through 7

Pursuit

After fasting and praying, Esther took action (Esther 5:1). She entered into the inner courts without an invitation and the king extended his scepter to her, which allowed her to come in to see him. God granted her favor with the king.

Not only did the king allow her to come to him, but he said he would give her whatever she asked for, even if it was half of the kingdom. Wow! Three times the king gave this response (Esther 5:3, 6; 7:2).

In the midst of all of this happening, God lifted up Mordecai, also giving him favor with the king. What's even more amazing is Haman (the one who plotted to kill the Jews in the first place) was the person who had to honor Mordecai. Talk about your enemies becoming your footstool—this is a perfect example. I believe that this happened as a result of fasting and prayer. Because the Jews trusted God for deliverance, fasted, and prayed, God answered their prayers.

What has happened in your life as a result of prayer and fasting?

_____
_____
_____
_____
_____
_____
_____

Pursuit

Haman's consequences of his sin and plot to destroy the Jews backfired; he and his ten sons were put to death. Because King Xerxes favored Queen Esther and promoted Mordecai, he gave them permission to write a letter in his name and send it to all the provinces to stop Haman's evil plot. As a result of their prayers and fasting, God honored their request. As we study the entire book of Esther, it seems that she was indeed made queen for "such a time as this." She was properly positioned to help her people. God's pursuit of her led her to the right place at the right time.

What has God positioned you for at this time? Consider where you are now. Where do you have influence? Is there someone in your life who needs to know Jesus as their Savior?

_____
_____
_____
_____
_____
_____
_____
_____
_____
_____
_____
_____

Pursuit

The book of Esther reminds us that we may not know or understand what God is doing and what He may be positioning us for; however, we can prepare by continually studying His Word, praying, and fasting.

Pursuit

And_____ in the Spirit on all occasions with all kinds of prayers and requests. With this in mind, be alert and always keep on praying for all the Lord's people. (Ephesians 6:18 NIV)

But when you ask, you must _____ and not _____, because the one who doubts is like a wave of the sea, blown and tossed by the wind. (James 1:6 NIV)

Do nothing out of _____ or vain conceit. Rather, in humility value others above _____, not looking to your _____ interests but each of you to the interests of the others. (Philippians 2:3-4 NIV)

For it is _____ who _____ in you to will and to act in order to fulfill his good purpose. (Philippians 2:13 NIV)

He _____ my soul. He _____ me along the right paths for his name's sake. (Psalm 23:3 NIV)

Mary and Joseph

Read: Luke 1

Meditational thought: The miraculous story of Jesus' birth is evidence of God's pursuit of me.

Jesus' parents, Mary and Joseph, were pursued by God like none other. They had to be special if God chose them to parent the Messiah, our Savior, here on earth. Can you imagine how their lives were changed when Jesus was born, or even throughout His life? How Mary was transformed after His death and His resurrection? There's a popular song titled, "Mary, Did You Know?" There are many renditions of this song, but I've never heard it sung quite like Miss Shellery sang it (she sang in the choir of the church that I grew up attending). The lyrics are deep and thought-provoking. Did Mary understand the magnitude of what was happening when the angel first appeared to her?

If you've never heard, "Mary, Did You Know?" take a moment to look it up online and listen to it. Write your thoughts here.

Pursuit

Luke 1:26–38 gives an account of the angel Gabriel appearing to Mary and delivering the news that she would conceive and give birth to a son. God isn't sending angels to us to tell us that we'll miraculously conceive, but God still pursues us and speaks to us in different ways.

What is one way you received a message from God that you didn't expect? What was the message?

Pursuit

There had to be a myriad of thoughts running through Mary's mind and questions she couldn't formulate (she was a teenager), but she didn't allow any of that to stand in the way of accepting what the angel said to her. In fact, her response, as detailed in Luke 1:38 (NLT) was, "I am the Lord's servant. May everything you have said about me come true." One thing we can learn from Mary here is to be open about what God is doing in our lives, especially when it looks nothing like anything we've done in the past, or anything we've known anyone else to do. In Mary's case, God had a miraculous plan. The events of the New Testament take place four hundred years after the final events of the Old Testament. King David was alive roughly a thousand years before the birth of Jesus, and God promised him that a descendant from the line of David would always sit on the throne of Israel (1 Kings 9:5).

Fast forward to Luke 1:27. The Bible tells us that Mary was engaged to Joseph, a descendant of King David. Jesus being born from the womb of Mary, who would be married to a descendant of King David, was not a coincidence, but rather intentional and part of God's plan. If you think for a moment that God gave up on planning after the time of the New Testament, think again. You and I are important to God as well and we all fit into His master plan of drawing all people unto Him. So, rest assured that you have been chosen and appointed for a specific task. The gifts that God have placed in you fit into His plan for your life, only you need to seek Him for the journey.

→Read Matthew 1

Pursuit

Joseph, on the other hand, didn't initially take the news of Mary's pregnancy well. In Matthew 1:19, Joseph decided he would end the engagement quietly, so that he wouldn't publicly disgrace her. Joseph didn't believe that Mary was miraculously pregnant, and so he wanted to end things and not be party to whatever Mary had going on, but God stepped in. He sent an angel to explain things to Joseph. Matthew 1:20–25 says,

As he considered this, an angel of the Lord appeared to him in a dream. "Joseph, son of David," the angel said, "do not be afraid to take Mary as your wife. For the child within her was conceived by the Holy Spirit. And she will have a son, and you are to name him Jesus, for he will save his people from their sins." All of this occurred to fulfill the Lord's message through his prophet: "Look! The virgin will conceive a child! She will give birth to a son, and they will call him Immanuel, which means 'God is with us.'" When Joseph woke up, he did as the angel of the Lord commanded and took Mary as his wife. But he did not have sexual relations with her until her son was born. And Joseph named him Jesus.

Joseph no longer contemplated leaving Mary, but instead he did just as the angel had commanded him and took Mary as his wife. Joseph had many a reason to be skeptical—a pregnant virgin and she was his wife! However, whether he was still confused or completely understood, he trusted and obeyed God.

Imagine the change that took place in Joseph's heart after Jesus was born and people came to praise Jesus and bring Him gifts. Or even the fact that an angel appeared to him again after Jesus was born, warning him to leave and flee to Egypt because Herod was planning to search for Jesus to kill Him. Later, an angel appeared to Joseph letting him know that it was safe to return to Israel. A third time an angel appeared to him redirecting his family to Nazareth.

We don't know what Joseph's relationship was like with God before Mary and her miraculous pregnancy, but he had to have some faith to trust God enough to marry Mary. But my how his faith must have grown after Jesus' birth! Angels appeared to him! God was literally guiding his footsteps and telling him where to go. We often pray and ask God to guide our steps, but will we have enough faith to move?

Have you been praying for God to guide you in making an important decision? What is your prayer? Has God answered?

_____
_____
_____
_____
_____
_____
_____
_____
_____
_____
_____
_____
_____

Pursuit

How do you think Joseph's encounters with the angel affected him spiritually?

_____
_____
_____
_____

Can you recall a personal encounter with God that has forever impacted your faith?

_____
_____
_____
_____
_____
_____
_____
_____
_____

Some of us may think of angels as people glowing and dressed in beautiful white robes, and if that's what we're looking for, we can surely miss God. God still speaks through dreams, but perhaps not in a way that we'd expect.

Pursuit

A few years ago, I kept a journal and pen next to my bedside so that I could jot down any dreams that came to me the night before. Every now and again, I would wake up when the dream was over in the middle of the night to write it down. I didn't want to miss anything that God may have been speaking to me. The next morning, I would read my note and most of the time it would be some crazy, illogical thing, but every now and again, it would be the answer I sought. Now, I'm not suggesting that you wake up in the middle of the night; I only did it because I was at the point where I was having very vivid dreams and I couldn't remember them the next morning. But what I am suggesting is that you find out what works for you. If you need to do that, then do it.

→Read 1 John 4

God still speaks through Scriptures, sermons, and dreams, though speaking through dreams is rare. I encourage you to be receptive. If you're unsure, God's Word says to "try the Spirit, by the Spirit" (1 John 4:1–5). If it isn't in alignment with God's Word, you can automatically scratch that. God will never lead you to do anything that is contrary to His character and His Word.

As you study Mary and Joseph's story, are you convinced of God's love and divine plan for you as well?

_____
_____
_____

Pursuit

What about their story convinces you of this truth?

Pursuit

_____ is she who has _____ that the Lord would fulfill his promises to her! (Luke 1:45 NIV)

My soul glorifies the Lord and my spirit rejoices in God my Savior, for he has been _____ of the humble state of his servant. From now on all generations will call me blessed, for the Mighty One has done _____ for me—holy is his name.. (Luke 1:47-49 NIV)

You, dear children, are from God and have overcome them, because the one who is in you is _____ than the one who is in the world. (1 John 4:4 NIV)

If anyone _____ that Jesus is the Son of God, God _____ in them and they in God (1 John 4:15 NIV)

For to us a child is born, to us a son is given, and the government will be on his shoulders. And he will be called _____. (Isaiah 9:6 NIV)

And afterward, I will _____ out my _____ on all people. Your sons and daughters will prophesy, your old men will dream dreams, your young men will see visions. Even on my servants, both men and women, I will pour out my _____ in those days. (Joel 2:28–29 NIV)

She will give birth to a son, and you are to give him the name Jesus, because he will _____ his people from _____. (Matthew 1:21 NIV)

Jesus' disciples

Read: Matthew 4:18–25

Meditational thought: By faith, I can follow Jesus.

Matthew 4 gives a short account of Jesus selecting His first four disciples: Peter, Andrew, James, and John. And by short, I really mean short. Jesus was walking along the shores of the sea of Galilee when He called out to Peter and Andrew. They were fishermen who were out in boats casting their nets into the water when Jesus called to them and said to follow Him and He'd show them how to be fishers of men. What caught my attention is that they immediately stopped what they were doing to follow Him. As far as we know, according to what is written, they didn't question Him. By faith Peter and Andrew followed Him, even if they weren't sure what He meant by "fishers of men." By faith James and John immediately followed Jesus when He first called. In fact, James and John left their boat and father behind to follow Jesus.

What is the last thing you did by faith even if you didn't understand why God was leading you in that direction?

_____
_____
_____
_____
_____
_____
_____
_____

Do you respond immediately in faith as James and John did, when God is leading you to take action? Why or why not?

_____
_____
_____
_____
_____
_____
_____
_____

Pursuit

What habits, ideals, people, routines, etc. are you willing to leave behind to follow Jesus?

_____

_____

_____

_____

_____

_____

_____

God often calls us to action. Our excuses lead to our delayed obedience or complete disobedience. At the time Jesus called His first disciples, His ministry was just beginning. Even if they didn't know much about Him, they wanted to know more and showed their desire by following Him. From this we learn that even if we are babes in Christ, we should still follow Him and trust Him. Most importantly, God wants our trust and obedience. This doesn't mean that along your spiritual journey you won't have problems, but you will have Jesus along with you, leading you into God's loving arms.

After calling the first four disciples, Jesus began teaching them and the many others who chose to follow Him. Likewise, when we're obedient to the call of God to follow Him, He leads us in His Word, teaching us His ways and how to love people the way Jesus did. Jesus handpicked His disciples; He chose them by name.

Pursuit

You have been chosen as well and God desires to work in your life, teaching you more about Him, growing you in your faith so that you can be sent out to be a vessel for Him. Notice that Jesus taught His disciples many things about the kingdom of God before He sent them out on their own.

→Read Matthew 10

In Matthew 10, Jesus sent His twelve disciples to the people of Israel with specific instructions to warn them that the kingdom of God is near, cure those with leprosy, cast out demons, heal their sick, and raise their dead. These are all things that Jesus had been doing, and also teaching them all the while after He called them to follow Him. He did not send them without knowledge or authority. They were equipped with what they needed. He even commanded them not to take money for their journey, but to find worthy people and stay in their homes.

When God pursues you, He is concerned about you receiving the most important thing for your journey—Him. The more you spend time with Him, the more you will become aware of your assignment He has given you. No matter what that assignment is, the end result is the same: to lift up the kingdom of God and to help draw others closer to Him.

Peter, the first of the twelve disciples, spent much time in Jesus' presence, learning His ways. Because of the time spent with Jesus, his faith was great, though it faltered a couple of notable times, once when he walked on water and again when he denied knowing Jesus three times before Jesus' death on the cross. However, Peter bounced back and taught and healed many people in Jesus' name. Peter also wrote two books of the Bible. From the moment Jesus called Peter, He knew that Peter would slip up from time to time, yet that didn't make Jesus change His mind about choosing Peter. Jesus knew the transformation that would take place in Peter's life because of the time spent in His presence. And as God is all knowing and the same today as He was during biblical times, He knows the transformation that will take place in your life as well.

Write a prayer of repentance for the sin that holds you back from pursuing the assignment that God has given you.

_____
_____
_____
_____
_____
_____
_____
_____
_____
_____
_____
_____
_____
_____

Pursuit

God has chosen you, right where you are, to draw others to Him. As you read this chapter, who did God reveal to you who needs Jesus?

_____

_____

_____

_____

→ Read Acts 2

After Jesus' death, resurrection, and ascension to heaven, the believers were filled with the Holy Spirit. In Acts 2, we see how the Holy Spirit empowered believers, causing them to speak in tongues (different languages). The Holy Spirit also used Peter as a vessel to preach the Gospel (good news of Jesus Christ) and heal the sick. When the people from other areas heard the believers speaking in tongues, the nonbelievers called them drunk (Acts 2:13); however, Peter used that as an opportunity to preach the Good News. You may be ridiculed, ignored, or cast out when you're doing something against the norm, contrary to what the crowd is doing, following Jesus. Oftentimes what the Spirit is leading you to do will not look like the world and it may feel like you're alone; it'll also be uncomfortable. However, even in the midst of your discomfort and loneliness, the God of comfort (Isaiah 40:1–11) is with you, leading you along the best path for your life and the glory of the kingdom (Psalm 32:8).

Pursuit

As a result of Peter's obedience to the Holy Spirit and willingness to be a vessel, Acts 2:41 tells us that about three thousand people were saved that day. Peter may not have known that many people would become believers in that moment, and often we don't know what the impact of our actions will be.

→Read Romans 14

I encourage you to listen to the voice of the Holy Spirit and obey His promptings. Who will get to experience God because of your obedience? Who will be saved because you allowed the Holy Spirit to work through you? Thoughts like these may carry a heavy burden or may seem like they're too much, but that is the kingdom mindset that God wants us to have. Whether we like it or not, our actions affect others, and sometimes that could result in whether or not one person wants to know Jesus.

Have you given much consideration to how you impact God's people? Why or why not? If so, how do your choices and actions reflect your consideration?

_____
_____
_____
_____
_____
_____

Pursuit

_____
_____
_____

Can you recall an interaction with someone that could have led them to Jesus, but did the opposite? Is there anything you would do/say differently today?

_____
_____
_____
_____
_____
_____
_____

But Peter said, "I don't have any silver or gold for you. But I'll give you what I have. In the name of Jesus Christ the Nazarene, get up and walk!" (Acts 3:6)

What a powerful statement! In fact, it is so powerful that the man is healed and begins to walk (after not being able to walk for nearly forty years as we find in subsequent verses). What I love about this is Peter gave what he had. What did he have? The power of the Holy Spirit at work within him. Faith. Love. Compassion. Because Peter gave what he had, this man was healed and became a believer in Jesus Christ. Those who witnessed that this man was now healed were amazed, so Peter used it as an opportunity to speak to the crowd about Jesus, leading thousands more to salvation.

Give what you have. Giving doesn't always equate to things of monetary value, but to the gifts and fruit of the Spirit within you. First Corinthians 12, 13, and 14 gives a great explanation of spiritual gifts. If you're unsure of what your gifts are, many resources are available to help you discover that (along with prayer and time alone in God's presence, the greatest resource). You can learn to use what you have for the edification of the kingdom. Your gifts have the potential to draw many to Christ.

Do you know your spiritual gifts? Are you actively using them for the edification of God's kingdom?

_____
_____
_____
_____
_____
_____
_____
_____
_____

Pursuit

If you do not know your spiritual gifts, or if you aren't using your spiritual gifts, will you commit to seek them and use them for the edification of God's kingdom? Write your prayer of commitment here.

_____
_____
_____
_____
_____
_____
_____
_____

→Read Acts 4

Acts 4:13 gives us powerful insight. Oftentimes we perceive those who are out front, visible, preaching, teaching, or doing some other notable service as greater than ourselves, yet they are ordinary people. We are all ordinary people, but we are distinguished or set apart when we spend time with God by reading and studying His Word and gaining insight through prayer. There is an outward manifestation in our lives when we spend time with Jesus. Others will recognize it as the council could see in Acts 4:13. It will be evident in how we talk, how we act, what we do, the choices we make, and how we treat others. No special training required, only love and time with Jesus, and we too can impact the kingdom of Christ.

Another thing that's clearly important as a believer is community with other believers. (See Acts 2:42–47 and Acts 4:32–37.) Though following God can be a narrow and lonely road in today's society, you're not meant to travel alone. Psalm 133 encourages us in the concept that unity is beautiful. Some of our churches can become so large that we get lost in the shuffle, but God doesn't want that for us. Many churches have embraced the concept of small groups, which are members of the church who connect and meet on a weekly (or regular) basis to build relationships. If this concept is new to you, I'd like to encourage you to start your own group of people who share similar interests so that you may have a source of encouragement and community in your daily walk with Christ. As Proverbs teaches us, "Iron sharpens iron," and we all could benefit from sharpening as we grow in Jesus Christ.

Do you belong to a small group of some kind? How has it been beneficial to you?

_____
_____
_____
_____
_____
_____
_____

Pursuit

If you're not part of a small group, will you commit to joining or creating one to further your walk with Christ?

_____
_____
_____
_____
_____
_____
_____
_____

Pursuit

And the very hairs on your head are all _____. So don't be afraid; you are more valuable to God than a whole flock of sparrows. (Luke 12:7)

_____ other believers who are weak in faith, and don't argue with them about what they think is right or wrong. (Romans 14:1)

How wonderful and pleasant it is when brothers live together in _____. (Psalm 133:1)

I will praise thee; for I am fearfully and _____ made: marvelous are thy works; and that my soul knoweth right well. (Psalm 139:14 KJV)

You saw me before _____. Every day of my life was recorded in your book. _____ was laid out before a single day had passed. (Psalm 139:16)

How precious are your thoughts about me, O God. They cannot be _____. (Psalm 139:17)

All the believers devoted themselves to the apostles' teaching, and to _____, and to sharing in meals (including the Lord's Supper), and to prayer. (Acts 2:42)

Me

Read: Luke 15

Meditational thought: How has God pursued me?

As I contemplate the idea of God constantly in pursuit of me, I have vivid memories as far back as first or second grade. I remember a conversation I had with a friend while walking home. It was quite silly, as you can imagine a conversation between seven-year-olds who are trying to find their place in the world could be. We were discussing who we were "down" with. This was a conversation that we'd been having over several days, but until this particular day, my friend had always given a different response. Mind you, I didn't even know what it was to be "down" in the first place, but it was silly conversation that kids my age were having about things like colors, either blue or red. Unexpectedly, my friend said that she was down with G.O.D. (She spelled it out.)

It didn't occur to me what she meant because up until that point, we'd only discussed colors. Confused, I asked, "What's that?"

Pursuit

She emphatically responded, "God!" And going right along with her, I agreed that I was also *down with God.*

At this age, my knowledge of and experience with God was limited, but I believed He existed. My family and I didn't attend weekly church services at that time in my life, but there was a seed of faith in me. Around the age of eight, my grandmother gave me a small Bible that contained a New Testament and the book of Psalms. I yearned to know more and that could only be attributed to God pursuing me. I picked up that Bible to read from time to time, but didn't understand a thing, yet that didn't stop me from wanting to know more.

Throughout the years, God used many of my friends (mainly those who attended church regularly) to speak encouragement to me, reminding me that He was there.

Your circle of friends is important to your spiritual growth. What we have to remember is that we are influenced by our relationships. Who do you want it to be, and what is the influence you want to have?

In junior high, I recall my social studies teacher, Mrs. Williams, assigning poems for us to perform in class. I don't recall the occasion, but I do remember being nervous. Of all the poems she assigned, mine was quite different. It was the Crucifixion. Now, I wasn't saved at this time and my knowledge of Jesus, His life, death, and resurrection, was slim. When the time came to recite our assigned poems, I was nervous as I am most of the time when I have to stand in front of a crowd to speak. That particular time, it worked to my advantage. My nervousness came across as great emotion and my teacher loved it! I'm not sure why she chose me to do that particular piece, but I believe that was all part of God's pursuit of me. Though a couple of years passed after that moment before God saved me, I learned a little more about Jesus' death because of that assignment.

In Luke 15:7, the Bible reassures us that there is rejoicing in Heaven when one sinner repents and turns to God. From sixth grade through part of my senior year in high school, I played the flute. I loved the band and the other students I'd come to know from being a part of such a community. As soon as I got the chance, I put down the flute and picked up the baton to become a majorette. Being a part of the band was my favorite high school experience and what helped mold me into the person I am today. In band practice, in ninth grade, an older student asked me if I was saved. I had no idea what he meant, and he only gave me a brief explanation, yet he planted a seed. Now that I think about it, it was the strangest random interaction. He walked up to me in the middle of a break and said, "Natasha, are you saved?" My expression must have told him my answer and he then asked if I'd been baptized, to which I responded no. He then looked me square in the eyes and said, "Well then you're going to hell!" And with that, he walked away, leaving me to chew on his words.

I'm not sure why he chose me, because it didn't seem as if he'd asked anyone else. Maybe a leader at church challenged the youth to share Christ and that's the way he chose to do it. At any rate, I thought I was a rather good kid. Respectful to adults. I helped others when I could. Earned good grades, excelling at the top of my class, and yet this kid tells me I'm going to hell. Wasn't I good enough not to go? Didn't God see my good deeds? It was also around this time that my mom started taking me to church regularly again and my interest in Jesus' salvation heightened. I soon learned that my good deeds meant nothing if I hadn't accepted Jesus Christ as my Lord and Savior, believing that He died on the cross for my sins, God raised Him from the dead, and confessing this truth with my mouth. I then followed Jesus through baptism the following summer. I didn't know it at the time, but now I clearly see that God pursued me through my fellow band member and I'm forever thankful.

Can you recall the moment God began pursuing you to salvation?

_____
_____
_____
_____
_____
_____
_____
_____

If you have not accepted Jesus as your Lord and Savior, you may do so now. I believe that God is pursuing your heart through this book. To receive salvation, you must accept that Jesus is Lord, believe that He died on the cross for your sins and that God raised Him from the dead, and confess this truth with your mouth. Study Romans 3:21–31. If you

Pursuit

accepted Jesus into your heart right now, let me be the first to congratulate you on your step of faith! Find a church home where you can learn more about God and grow in your faith.

God's pursuit of us doesn't end at the moment we're saved from eternal separation from Him; He continues to pursue us so that we may get to know Him, and draw closer to Him, and become more like Him.

When you're saved, God pursues you through His Holy Word (the Bible), prayer, circumstances, and sermons (messages from the pastor). God's pursuit of you may not always be evident in the moment; as we know, hindsight is 20/20. Oftentimes, we have to look back to see that God was after our hearts in a particular situation, steering us on the right path.

I recall my first couple of weeks in college. Fresh out of my parents' nest and on my own for the first time in my life. Scary yet exciting. Incoming freshmen were allowed to move into the dorms about a week or so before classes started, which gave us plenty of time to socialize. Once classes began, I attempted to keep the same level of socialization going, but the new friend I'd made quickly reminded me that she wasn't majoring in plaziology 101 (the plaza was the center of campus where all the fun activities took place). After she told me she wouldn't leave the dorm with me to hang out, I decided not to go. I wasn't extroverted enough to go alone. Her proclamation was a reminder to me as well. She may never have known how her words/actions that evening impacted me, nor will she likely know that God used her to keep me on track. But how much differently my college experience could have turned out had she fed into my excitement of newfound freedom. As time passed God placed other students, whom I now have as friends for nearly twenty years, in my path to help me remain focused.

We can be influenced, sometimes subtly, by those around us, and I'm thankful that God pursued me through some of my most impressionable years.

God's pursuit of us is evident through relationships with children, spouse, and sermons. In what current situation do you recognize God's pursuit of you?

_____

_____

_____

_____

_____

_____

_____

Even today when I deal with tough situations, it is a reminder to shift my focus to my heavenly Father. Does that mean I ignore the issue? No. But it does mean that I focus on my Creator instead of the issues that come to shift my focus. Every now and then, life can deal some pretty tough situations, often those that are beyond our control, but we must choose how we will deal with them. We can study God's Word, pray, seek wise counsel, and take action within our control. The rest? We must trust that God will see us through it. We must choose not to be consumed by our troubles. Even in the midst of uncertainty, (such as now as I write this, our nation deals with the rapid spread of the coronavirus, or COVID-19), we can use it as an opportunity to grow close to God, and even help others when it's in our power to do so. The question we must ask ourselves is, how is God pursuing me through this?

Be More Like Him

The ultimate goal in our Christian walk while here on earth is to be like Christ: having the mind of Christ, loving like Christ (selflessly), and being like Him (full of compassion). In every situation, we have a choice to make. Will we respond like Christ or allow our emotions to take over? In traffic? To the co-worker who undermines us? The boss who doesn't seem to value our work? The children who drive us insane? The church member who gossips about us? The person who lied about us? The list goes on. Every day throughout the day, we must choose. After we say yes to Christ for salvation, we have to say yes to Him and His ways each day. The daily yes isn't always easy, but when we choose *no* by doing or saying something that contradicts God's Word, we'll be convicted by it, because God is in pursuit of our whole heart. He wants a daily yes from you and me.

If you've been in a place of perpetual no and you're ready to give God your *yes* again, know that as in Luke 15 in the parables of the lost sheep, lost coin, and lost son, heaven rejoices at your return to the Father.

Pursuit

"'My son,' the father said, 'you are always with me, and _____ I have is yours. But we had to celebrate and be glad, because this brother of yours was _____ and is alive again; he was _____ and is _____.'" (Luke 15:31-32 NIV)

I tell you that in the same way there will be more rejoicing in heaven over _____ sinner who repents than over ninety-nine righteous persons who do not need to repent. (Luke 15:7 NIV)

The Lord is not _____ in keeping his promise, as some understand slowness. Instead he is _____ with you, not wanting anyone to perish, but _____ to come to repentance. (2 Peter 3:9 NIV)

For the kind of sorrow God wants us to experience leads us _____ _____. There's no regret for that kind of sorrow. But worldly sorrow, which lacks repentance, results in spiritual death. (2 Corinthians 7:10 NLT)

Dear Reader,

I hope this Bible study has encouraged you to look within and find God moving in your life in ways you hadn't recognized before now. It is my sincere hope that you know and cherish the fact that God loves you and wants to have a relationship with you regardless of what's happening in your life.

Take a moment and let me know what you think of the study! Reach out to me on social media or e-mail.

Facebook - @craves.2012

Website – www.natashafrazier.com

E-mail – natasha@natashafrazier.com

Instagram - @author_natashafrazier

Twitter - @author_natashaf

Natasha

Pursuit

Please enjoy this excerpt from *How Long Are You Going to Wait*

SEEK GOD FOR PURPOSE

Because our purpose comes from God, it is important to first seek God for what it is that He desires for you in this season of your life. If you believe that God has given you a vision, it is only right to seek Him first. You see, you may know your purpose, but how you should be carrying it out may be different than how you carried it out last year or how you will need to carry it out a few years from now, and that can cause some level of uncertainty. But our Master knows and can provide the answers for which you seek, this is why I believe it is important that we are in constant prayer and communication with God to seek His will.

Psalm 37:4 tells us that God will give us the desires of our heart if we delight ourselves in Him. In order to delight in Him, we must learn more about Him and that is done by spending time in His presence. When we spend time in His presence, inevitably, our desires will begin to match His. Our desires must be in alignment with God's will; it is at this time that God will give us the desires of our heart.

Seeking God: What does this look like? Begin with praying and asking God to show you what He wants you to do. I can attest that the Lord will show you if you truly desire so and make yourself available to do His will. Have you already begun praying about it? Can you recall the answers that God has given you, if any? Do you recognize God's voice?

Not only is it important to pray about purpose but it is imperative that we know how to identify God's voice. How does God speak? I have learned that God speaks through scripture and that clarity is given through prayer, and oftentimes through His messengers. When you're concerned about whether or not God is speaking to you, remember two things: God always gives confirmation and God will never move you to do anything that is contrary to His Word and His character.

Study the following scriptures: John 10, 1 Samuel 3; Isaiah 30:21; John 16:13

Application

1. Write down a specific prayer asking God to show you what it is He desires you to do in this season of your life.

2. John 10 speaks about God's sheep being able to discern His voice. Do you have problems with discerning God's voice?

3. In 1 Samuel 3, Samuel was just learning God's voice. Note that Samuel was alone. Do you allow yourself to be alone and in a place where there are no distractions so that you can hear God's voice clearly?

4. Choose a time to seek God alone and meditate on His word. Be as specific as possible. God will honor the time that you establish to meet Him.

5. What are some things that hinder you from hearing God's voice clearly? (worries, desires of others, fear, etc)

6. Be honest with yourself and God. Be willing to sacrifice your time.

Ask yourself:

1. Do I truly desire to walk in the purpose that God has for me?

2. What am I willing to sacrifice? (Think temporary satisfaction for the pursuit of purpose)

3. Are my prayers for purpose specific?

4. In what ways has God answered your prayers to show you your assignments? What actions of faith did you take when God revealed His assignment for your life?

LIFE IS CHOICE DRIVEN

Its one thing to have a vision, goal or dream that you want to achieve but it's another thing to actually pursue it. Far too often, we all walk around with ideas buried inside of us and choose not to make them a reality because of fear of the unknown, what others may think of us or failure.

It is true. We do not know what the future holds but I can guarantee you that if you never do anything past just thinking or dreaming about your goals, you will never achieve them and in turn, fail.

The difference between those who achieve and those who do not is: choices. We simply have to take the necessary steps to move forward, allowing failure to be our teacher.

Those who know me well know that I talked about writing a book for many years before I actually had the guts to do it. I often think back to January 2009 when I actually put it on paper for the first time as a goal. It wasn't a clear measurable goal; my notepad simply said: Write a book. I was proud of myself too, thinking I had done something. In fact, in my mind, it was almost as if I'd written a book based on the level of excitement I had.

In January 2009, our pastor preached a series of sermons on purpose and "getting to your address," and my address was writing a book. Back during that time, our cameras often zoomed in on members of the congregation during worship service. I saw myself on one of the rollbacks of one particular service in January where we were instructed to bring our plans and the pastor would pray over them. I was standing near the front waving my notepad proudly.

I wrote a couple of pages but that was about the extent of it. I allowed so many other things to get in the way and that prevented me from completing my goal. I often think back to that moment because I had done nothing more than write down what I wanted to do with no plan as to how I was going to get there.

Write it Down

I believe it is very important to write down your goals. I'm not saying this just because I'm an author and enjoy writing; but I truly believe that writing helps the goal setter. Writing things down helps solidify and clarify your thoughts. Writing also holds you accountable.

Let me caution you not to do as I did back in 2009 and simply write your goal, but I encourage you to take it a step further and create actionable plans to help you accomplish this goal. Writing things like, "Start a business," is not going to help you accomplish your goal. Be specific. What kind of business do you want to start? What is it going to take for you to get your business running? What resources do you need? What research needs to be done? When are you going to start making strides to accomplish these things? Set a date.

Giving yourself a deadline is very important because it gives you something to work toward. Be as specific as possible but also be flexible. These are your goals and it is okay if you don't meet the exact dates that you originally set; make adjustments. The important thing here is that you are working toward bringing your vision to life and you are no longer just dreaming or thinking about it but you are making steps to make it a reality.

The Choice

Even though you may write it down, nothing will happen until you choose to pursue that which God has placed upon your heart. No one can make that decision for you and no one can pursue it on your behalf. Remember that the vision was given to you so it is up to you to see it to fruition.

Don't be intimidated or discouraged by the fact that everyone will not be excited about this new thing you're embarking upon. Don't even expect that. Don't allow the lack of excitement of others to keep you from being positive and moving with the same vigor you had when you decided to step out in faith to pursue it.

The Wait

There are several reasons why we procrastinate when it comes to living a life of purpose: concern with how big or small our assignment is, comparing ourselves to others, lack of counsel, time, or other resources, and fear. I will spend the rest of this book encouraging you not to let any of those things stop you and take action one step at a time to get to the place you're destined to be.

Study the following Scriptures: Habbakkuk 2, Hebrews 6:11, Proverbs 10:4, 12:24, 21:5, Psalm 119:173

Application

1. Write down the vision that God has given you.
2. What has stopped you from pursuing this vision?
3. How can you overcome these obstacles?
4. Create a list of actionable steps and goals (measurable, realistic, achievable, time-based) that will position you to achieve get to the place you're trying to go.

To purchase your copy of *How Long Are You Going to Wait*, please visit www.natashafrazier.com

www.ingramcontent.com/pod-product-compliance
Lightning Source LLC
Chambersburg PA
CBHW020428010526
44118CB00010B/469